WHEN Martin Luther King Jr. WORE ROLLER SKATES

by
Mark Weakland

Illustrated by
Patrick Ballesteros

PICTURE WINDOW BOOKS
a capstone imprint

When Martin Luther King Jr. was 8 years old, a woman in a department store lunged at him and slapped him.

"You stepped on my foot!" she yelled.

Martin didn't know the angry white woman standing in front of him, but he stayed calm. Although he was shocked, he simply walked away.

Martin was a child who learned to overcome difficulties without violence. Like his mother, he was gentle and caring. Like his father, he was determined and fearless. Martin drew on these childhood traits as he grew up. He became a leader admired by millions of people around the world.

It was January 15, 1929. In the hallway outside his bedroom, Martin Luther King Sr. nervously paced. His family called him Daddy King. Inside the bedroom his wife was giving birth. Daddy King leaped with joy when he found out that the baby was a boy. No one knew then that this small child would become a great man.

The Kings named their son Michael, after Daddy King. But a few years later, Daddy King changed both his name and his son's name to Martin.

Martin's parents gave him a wonderful life. He lived in a comfortable home. He had a younger brother and older sister to play with. And he had loving adults all around him, including his grandparents who lived in the same house.

Daddy King was a minister. His sermons and his interest in civil rights helped shape Martin's beliefs early on.

Martin's mother taught him to believe in himself. "You are as good as anyone," she said.

In Martin's family church was an important part of life. Once his father hosted a guest preacher from Virginia. The man talked to folks about joining the church. Martin's sister was the first one to sign up. When he saw her joining, little Martin decided to join too.

"You're only 5 years old!" said the preacher.

"I'm not going to let my sister get ahead of me," Martin said. "I'm joining next!"

Martin's family lived in a 12-room house on Auburn Avenue in Atlanta, Georgia. The house was the center of Martin's universe. In the backyard he played with kids from the neighborhood. He roller skated and biked up and down Auburn Avenue with his friends.

At school Martin got along with the other children. But there was a school bully. When that bully hit him, Martin refused to fight back. He knew violence was not the answer.

Martin's brother was named Alfred Daniel, but everyone called him A.D. He and Martin loved to run and play. They played football and baseball. And they played basketball at the fire station near their house. Because of racial segregation, no black men or women worked there. But at the station, kids of different races all played together.

Every evening the Kings sat down to eat dinner together. Martin's father insisted that no one eat until he got home.

When Daddy King got home late, the kids were starving. But still they couldn't eat. First they had to recite a Bible verse. The boys were smart. The verse they often picked was just two words—Jesus wept.

"It's the shortest verse in the Bible," said Martin with a grin.

Martin often played with a boy from the neighborhood. It didn't matter to Martin that the boy was white. The two of them were good friends.

One day the boy's father told his son that he could no longer play with Martin. Martin did not understand why the boys couldn't be friends.

"Why?" he asked Daddy King. "Why did his father say we can't play together?"

Martin's parents talked to him about race and segregation. They told him that black people were often treated terribly. Martin was shocked. He decided he should hate white people.

"You should not hate the white man. It's your duty as a Christian to love him," said his parents.

Martin had a hard time understanding this. "How can I love a race of people who hate me and who are responsible for breaking me up with one of my best childhood friends?" he asked.

"You must try," said his mother.

"One day I'll change things," said Martin. "One day I'm going to turn this world upside down."

Martin was determined. He felt angry when he experienced discrimination because of the color of his skin.

When he was 14 years old, Martin traveled on a bus with a teacher to a speech contest. On the way home, Martin and his teacher were forced out of their seats so whites could take them. It was a 90-mile (145-kilometer) trip. Martin and his teacher stood for three hours on that ride home.

Martin later said, "It was the angriest I have ever been in my life."

Martin was very smart. He skipped right over the ninth and eleventh grades. By age 15 Martin started college!

In college Martin was popular. But he wasn't sure about the rest of his life. He had always thought he would become a minister like his father. But he began to question his faith. Eventually, though, he came back to his roots.

"I have decided to lead a church," he told his father.

By the time Martin was 25 years old, he had earned a doctoral degree. He married Coretta Scott. Like Martin, she believed in the importance of peace. The couple settled in Montgomery, Alabama, and had four children.

Martin's parents were proud when he became pastor of the Dexter Avenue Baptist Church. His father, Daddy King, was especially happy.

As Martin grew older, he became more active in helping African Americans gain rights. He was chosen to be the spokesperson for the Montgomery Bus Boycott in 1955. Later he led non-violent actions, including sit-ins, demonstrations, and marches for civil rights. He said that he would not respond to violence with violence.

Martin gave some of the most memorable speeches in American history. In 1963 he gave his famous "I have a dream" speech before 200,000 people in Washington, D.C.

In his speech Martin said, "I have a dream that my four little children will one day live in a nation where they will not be judged by the color of their skin but by the content of their character."

AFTERWORD

Throughout his life, Martin Luther King Jr. fought peacefully for civil rights. He also focused on helping the poor and on world peace. In 1964 Martin received the Nobel Peace Prize for his efforts. In 1964 and 1965, he played an instrumental part in securing civil rights and voting rights for all African Americans.

In 1968 Martin Luther King Jr. was shot and killed in Memphis, Tennessee, at the age of 39. Throughout his life Martin Luther King Jr. held tight to the traits he developed as a young boy—gentleness, caring, fearlessness, and determination. By staying true to himself, he became a great American leader.

GLOSSARY

admire—to like and respect someone

boycott—to stop taking part in something to show support for an idea or group of people

civil rights—freedoms that every person should have; in the 1950s and 1960s, black Americans still did not have full civil rights; they led a civil rights movement to get the government to give them the rights they deserved

demonstration—a public meeting or march protesting something or expressing views on something

discrimination—treating people unfairly because of their race, country of birth, or gender

doctoral degree—the highest advanced degree earned by study and research at a college or university

minister—a person who leads a church

race—a major group into which humans can be divided; people of the same race share a physical appearance, such as skin color

recite—to say aloud something you memorized

segregation—separating people because of their skin color

sermon—a talk on a religious subject that is based on a bible verse

trait—a quality or characteristic that makes one person different from another

violence—hurting someone else with words or actions; yelling bad words and hitting are both violent actions

Jazynka, Kitson. *Martin Luther King, Jr.* National Geographic Readers. Washington, D.C.: National Geographic, 2012.

Meltzer, Brad. *I am Martin Luther King, Jr.* Ordinary People Change the World. New York: Dial Books for Young Readers, 2016.

Nelson, Kadir. *I Have a Dream.* New York: Schwartz & Wade Books, 2012.

CRITICAL THINKING WITH THE
★ COMMON CORE ★

1. A child's actions indicate the type of adult he or she will become. What did Martin Luther King Jr. do as a child that indicated what kind of adult he would become? Provide two examples and support your answer with words from the text. (Key Ideas and Details)

2. Martin Luther King Jr.'s family played an important rule in helping him become a great leader. What specific things did his family do that helped Martin become an exceptional man? Support your answer with two pieces of evidence from the text. (Integration of Knowledge and Ideas)

3. The author says, "Throughout his life, Martin Luther King Jr. held tight to the traits he developed as young boy—gentleness, caring, fearlessness, and determination." Link one or more of these early character traits to three accomplishments Martin achieved as a man. Tell how each trait or traits enabled Martin to do what he did. (Craft and Structure)

INTERNET SITES

FactHound offers a safe, fun way to find Internet sites
related to this book. All of the sites on FactHound have
been researched by our staff.
Here's all you do:
Visit www.facthound.com
Type in this code: 9781479596850

Super-cool stuff!

Check out projects, games, and lots more at
www.capstonekids.com

OTHER TITLES IN
★ THIS SERIES ★

INDEX

Special thanks to our adviser for her advice and expertise:
Akinyele Umoja, Department Chair and Full Professor
African-American Studies
Georgia State University, Atlanta, Georgia

Editor: Shelly Lyons
Designer: Russell Griesmer
Creative Director: Nathan Gassman
Production Specialist: Tori Abraham
The illustrations in this book were created digitally.

Editor's Note: Direct quotations in the main text are indicated by bold words.
Direct quotations are found on the following pages:
Page 6, line 8: King, Martin Luther. *The Autobiography of Martin Luther King, Jr.*, p. 4.
Page 18, line 10: Farris, Christine King. *My Brother Martin*, p. 26.
Page 20, line 8: *The Autobiography of Martin Luther King, Jr.*, p. 10.
Page 27, line 15: King, Martin Luther, Jr. [1963] "I Have a Dream" (speech).
U.S. National Archives and Records Administration. https://www.archives.gov/press/exhibits/dream-speech.pdf.

Picture Window Books are published by Capstone, 1710 Roe Crest Drive, North Mankato, Minnesota 56003 www.mycapstone.com

Library of Congress Cataloging-in-Publication Data
Names: Weakland, Mark, author. | Ballesteros, Patrick, illustrator.
Title: When Martin Luther King Jr. wore roller skates /
by Mark Weakland ; illustrated by Patrick Ballesteros.
Description: North Mankato, Minnesota : Capstone Picture Window Books, 2017.
| Series: Leaders doing headstands | Includes bibliographical references.
Identifiers: LCCN 2015050708| ISBN 9781479596850 (library binding) |
ISBN 9781515801375 (paperback) | ISBN 9781515801450 (ebook pdf)
Subjects: LCSH: King, Martin Luther, Jr., 1929-1968—Childhood and
youth—Juvenile literature. | African Americans—Biography—Juvenile
literature. | Civil rights workers—United States—Biography—Juvenile
literature. | Baptists—United States—Clergy—Biography—Juvenile
literature. | African Americans—Civil rights—History—20th
century—Juvenile literature.
Classification: LCC E185.97.K5 W43 2017 | DDC 323.092—dc23
LC record available at http://lccn.loc.gov/2015050708

Printed in the United States   5829